Original title:
Tropical Winds and Ocean Blues

Copyright © 2025 Creative Arts Management OÜ
All rights reserved.

Author: Vivienne Beaumont
ISBN HARDBACK: 978-1-80581-580-8
ISBN PAPERBACK: 978-1-80581-107-7
ISBN EBOOK: 978-1-80581-580-8

Embrace the Essence of the Salty Kisses

The seagulls squawk, a raucous band,
They steal my chips; isn't that grand?
A beach ball bounce, then a surfboard slide,
I'm upside down, still filled with pride.

The sun does shine, but oh, what heat!
I dance like a crab on my tired feet.
Sandy toes and a wobbly drink,
I spill it all, then laugh and wink.

A jellyfish floats by, what a sight!
I dodge and weave, oh what delight!
The waves crash loud, they tickle my soul,
While sunscreen fails to protect my mole.

Flip-flops flying, a race to the shore,
"Last one in is a rotten chore!"
I cannonball down with a splashy glee,
Now my hair's a disaster, oh woe is me!

Boundless Horizons of the Aqua Realm

The fish are smiling, they wave with glee,
I swear I saw one wink at me!
With snorkel gear looking quite absurd,
I might just let out a funny word.

The sunburn's fierce, like a lobster's glow,
I tried to swim, but fell on my toe.
Each wave a giggle, a tickling tease,
Salt in my eyes, oh what a breeze!

A hermit crab scuttles, all dressed in style,
Chasing a wave, it's gone for a while.
"Catch me if you can," it seems to say,
But here comes a wave to wash it away!

With coconut drinks that never stay full,
I spill and slosh, it's quite the hullabaloo!
We laugh and we cheer on this silly spree,
In a land where the sea just wants to be free!

Essence of the Salty Breeze

The seagull squawks with flair,
Waving its wings without a care.
It spots a chip, yes, it's true,
And claims it all, like a seagull do.

A boat drifts by, with a clown aboard,
His jokes float out, as he strums a chord.
The fish they laugh, oh what a sight,
Even the crabs join in, feeling light.

Dreaming Under a Mango Sky

A mango drops, and splats with glee,
Splashing juice upon just me.
Lime juice squirted, made me squeal,
A fruit fight's truth, it's quite surreal!

The sunset paints with reds and yellows,
While coconut cows chase all the fellows.
They bump their heads, what a scene,
Under the glow, it's a fruit-themed dream.

Chasing Shadows on the Golden Sands

Footprints dance like they got a tune,
While crabs do the shimmy beneath the moon.
A flip-flop thwacks, flies through the air,
It lands on a dog, causing a scare!

Waves tickle toes as they splash and play,
The sun lays low, ending the day.
A beach ball flies into a lifeguard's hat,
He grins wide, 'Hey, that's just my mat!'

Rhythms of the Aquamarine Sea

Jellyfish waltz, what a sight to see,
Dancing in currents, wild and free.
A dolphin dives with a somersault,
Looks up and shouts, 'Does that tickle, Paul?'

Shells gossip while the tide takes a peek,
Sharing the town's latest cheek-to-cheek.
An octopus juggles, what a feat,
Even the fish stop for a seat!

Whispers of the Coral Breeze

In the splash of waves, I trip and fall,
My flip-flops flying, I hear the call.
A crab scuttles by, with a sassy dance,
While I am trying to salvage romance.

Seaweed appears, like hair gone wild,
The sun's too bright for this grown-up child.
With shades askew, I wave at a fish,
Who gives me a wink, a salty swish.

Azure Dreams Beneath the Waves

My floaty is bright, a sight to behold,
But it's slippery, I'm told, too bold!
I glide on my back with style and grace,
Until a wave hits, oh, what a race!

A dolphin giggles, jumps, and splashes,
While I flail like a fish with panicked thrashes.
The ocean laughs, that merry sly tease,
As I swear I was meant just to seize!

Swaying Palms and Salty Air

The palm trees sway, they're having a talk,
I join the convo, but can't find the rock.
A coconut drops, lands right on my hat,
I think it just might be a sneaky plop brat!

I dance with the breeze, a loopy ballet,
My friends cheer me on, 'It's your tropical day!'
With sand in my shoes, I give it a whirl,
In this sandy circus, I'm just a whirlgirl.

The Rhythm of the Shoreline

The waves come crashing, what a loud thump,
I tried to dance, but I fell with a bump.
A seagull laughs, it knows my plight,
As I do the wave, not quite right!

The rhythm is wild, but I give it a go,
A conga line forms, and I'm in tow.
With every splash, my troubles fall away,
Under the sun, I'm here to play!

When the Monsoon Meets the Sun

Raindrops dance on sandy shores,
Seagulls giggle, what a chore.
Umbrellas flip and fly away,
While beach balls join the fray.

Sunshine peeks through dripping leaves,
The laughter grows, oh how it cleaves.
Flip-flops flopped in mud and glee,
Is it summer or a spouting spree?

Clouds and rays in wild pursuit,
Who will win? This fun dispute.
Sandy toes and soggy snacks,
Waves come crashing, laughter cracks.

So, gather 'round, let's raise a cheer,
For wacky weather all the year.
Mixing sun with pouring rain,
Beach days never feel mundane!

Vibrations of the Cerulean Waves

The waves all wobble with delight,
Like jelly dancing in the light.
Surfers bounce like popcorn flies,
But wipeouts lead to splashy sighs.

Fishies chuckle, swim and weave,
As sunburnt folks try to believe.
Sandy sandwiches and fizzy drinks,
Who's invited? All the blinks!

Crabs in shades, strutting along,
Cracking jokes, they must be strong.
Seaweed wigs and sandy shoes,
Beach fashion? No, just fun views!

Life's a splash, a silly joke,
With every tumble, laugh and poke.
So grab a float, let's make waves,
In this place where joy behaves!

Serenity on a Beach of Dreams

Coconuts drop like tiny bombs,
While sunbathers hum their soothing psalms.
Towel debates on who got tanned,
And snack runs always poorly planned.

The seafoam giggles at our feet,
Tickling toes like a playful greet.
Beach chairs tilt in hilarious falls,
While sunscreen flies and laughter calls.

Seashells whisper, secrets to behold,
Fishy tales that never get old.
In the shade, a nap may lure,
But seagulls peek for snacks, I'm sure!

So let's embrace the sandy quirks,
In this wonderland where laughter jerks.
Each moment soaked in sweet delight,
Turns everyday into delight-fueled flight!

Driftwood Stories Beneath the Sky

Driftwood sprawls like lazy cats,
Claiming space with wooden spats.
Shells adorn the sandy stage,
As crabs prepare for their next page.

Tales of pirates, lost and round,
Is there treasure? Just seashells found.
A coconut with a silly face,
Hums a tune in this sunny place.

Seagulls squack in their own rhyme,
Poking fun, oh, what a crime!
Shells a-chatter, giggling tease,
While we soak up the ocean breeze.

So come and join this feast of fun,
Where stories blend and laughter runs.
Beneath the vast and azure sky,
Driftwood dreams bubble as they fly!

The Allure of the Seagrass Whisper

In the grassy depths, fish prance,
With fins that wiggle, they take their chance.
Crabs in tuxedos, they scuttle with flair,
Chasing each other, without a care.

Starfish gossip, lounging like stars,
While bubbles pop, playing tiny guitars.
Eels make faces, all in good jest,
Playing hide and seek, they know they're the best.

Shells wear hats, on sandy shores,
As seagulls squawk with their antics and roars.
The seaweed sways with a giggling sound,
While flounders try to dance without making a pound.

Laughter echoes in the salty spray,
In this wacky world, the creatures play.
A fish in a bowtie might steal the show,
As the sun dips low, putting on a glow.

Radiant Dances of Fin and Flipper

Dolphins twirl in a splashy parade,
With flips and spins, a grand charade.
They laugh at the tide, doing the wave,
As fish join in, so bold and brave.

Penguins waddle, quite out of style,
Trying to surf with a quirky smile.
Seals play tag, plopping on rocks,
They grin and cheer, no ticking clocks.

Parrots caw with a pop and a sizzle,
While pufferfish puff, looking quite drizzled.
In a swirl of colors, they strut and prance,
Creating a hoot, making hearts dance.

Under the sun, there's a giggling show,
In the depths of laughter, joy overflows.
As fin meets flipper, they whirl with glee,
This wacky fin fest is all we need to see.

Currents of Joy Beneath the Stars

Moonlit waves shimmer with delight,
As fish tell secrets to the night.
Crabs throw parties, with snacks all around,
As fortune cookies, they jokingly found.

Octopuses juggle, their limbs all a whirl,
Creating a scene with each twist and twirl.
Turtles join in, bringing their groove,
To the light of the moon, they all move.

The jellyfish glow, a glowing delight,
Bobbing and swaying, a magical sight.
Sandcastles built by the tide's gentle hand,
As laughter echoes across the land.

With each gentle push, the waves bring cheer,
As creatures gather, without any fear.
Under the blanket of starlit skies,
Laughter erupts, as the sea's humor flies.

Hushed Secrets of Coral Gardens

Coral blooms whisper sweet little lies,
As fish play poker beneath the blue skies.
Clams hide treasures, with secrets to keep,
While gobies peek in, no need for sleep.

Anemones dance, waving in glee,
While clownfish giggle and sip on sea tea.
The shrimp play checkers, all in good fun,
With pranks galore, the games have begun.

Seahorses trot in their fanciest attire,
Floating together, hearts never tire.
Eels tell tales with twists and with spins,
In this quiet garden, the laughter begins.

Diving deep down, there's joy to be found,
In the hush of the garden, laughter resounds.
As colors collide in this magical space,
The secrets unfold with each splash and grace.

Lush Revelations in Hibiscus Hues

In a garden where the fruits all chat,
A pineapple wore a funny hat.
The mango laughed, oh what a sight,
While coconuts danced in sheer delight.

Beneath the sun, a lizard pranced,
Swaying along as if he danced.
He whispered secrets of the breeze,
And tickled all the lazy bees.

A parrot squawked with a cheeky grin,
Complaining loudly of his twin.
They fought for perch on a swaying tree,
While laughing at fish who just missed me.

At dusk, they gathered for stories bright,
Of moonlit chases and silly flight.
With hibiscus tea, they shared a jest,
In this garden blush, we're truly blessed.

Tales of Fishermen and Ocean Dreams

Two fishermen with nets so wide,
Caught every fish, or so they cried.
But every catch that set them free,
Was just a scrap of seaweed, whee!

With rods of bamboo and laughter loud,
They cast their lines, feeling proud.
Swapped fish tales as the gulls stuffed pie,
While the sea frowned, oh my, oh my!

One said, 'My fish was quite the size!'
The other replied, 'Just look at the flies!'
To the sound of waves, their laughter grew,
In a boat that once was bright, now blue.

At sunset, they fished out stories absurd,
Of the talking crab and the fish that heard.
With every cast, they lost their aim,
Yet found rich joy in a silly game.

Woven Stories from the Deep Blue

In a realm of foam where sea critters yawn,
A clam declared the sun's glow was gone.
The starfish laughed with a wobbly grin,
'That's just the tide, now come join in!'

A school of fish in a fancy parade,
Swam in circles, oh, what a charade!
With each flip, they hinted at a quest,
To find the seaweed that tasted best.

A turtle strolled, slow as could be,
Claiming wisdom from under the sea.
'Can we have wisdom without a chase?'
'Only if you're graceful, not at my pace!'

The jellyfish glimmered, dancing with glee,
While seahorses giggled, 'Look at me!'
In the depths, they spun tales so bright,
Weaved from laughter, pure ocean delight.

Radiance of the Moonlit Waters

When the moonbeam tickles the surf so light,
A crab in a tux strolled into the night.
He tipped his hat to a breeze so sly,
And winked to the fish that flitted by.

The waves giggled, showing their teeth,
As the shellfish sang of dreams beneath.
Tiny shrimp joined in the dreamy parade,
With puffs of bubbles, their joy relayed.

The dolphins jumped, flipping with flair,
While a whale told jokes from the depths of despair.
'Why don't fish play piano with style?'
'Cause they can't find their keys, not for a while!'

A night full of sparkles, fish tales galore,
Every giggle echoed from the ocean floor.
Under the stars, they danced till the dawn,
In waters that shimmered, we laughed on and on.

Serenade of the Sunlit Shore

Seagulls sing, with snack in beak,
A clam on the run, too fast to sneak.
Beach balls bouncing, sun hats fly,
As sandy toes wave goodbye.

Rinse my shorts in salty spray,
My ice cream's melting, oh what a way.
Flip-flops race, then trip and clash,
Surfboards topple—splash, crash, splash!

Children giggle, lost in the fray,
Crabs doing the cha-cha in the bay.
A dolphin's leap, the crowd goes wild,
Underneath the sun, we all feel like a child.

Flip flops echo, paths of fun,
Sandy castles—quick, we must run!
King of the beach, I claim my stake,
But oops! That throne's a jellyfish lake!

Lullabies of the Azure Deep

Fish with shades swim in a line,
Making waves, looking so fine.
A whale hums tunes, smooth as cream,
While sea turtles waddle in dream.

Octopus juggling shells on view,
Anemones wave, saying boo!
Starfish lounge as they sip on tea,
Pretending they're in a fancy spree.

Corals laugh with colors bright,
Clownfish tease, oh what a sight!
Dolphins play tag, diving with glee,
While I sip my drink by the sea.

Bubbles whisper secrets old,
Sharks in capes, oh so bold.
Underwater disco, the crabs all sway,
We dance in the deep, come join the play!

Secrets Beneath the Palms

Coconuts giggle with a crack,
While squirrels plan a nutty attack.
Palm fronds rustle a secret song,
Oh, flip-flop fashion! You can't go wrong!

Lizards pose, fashionably bright,
Chasing shadows, giving a fright.
A iguana wears shades, think he's cool,
But is he just the neighborhood fool?

Grapes on the grill—who thought that was fun?
Tropical fruit salad, here comes the sun!
Lemons get juiced, oh what a fuss,
While pineapples chant, 'In us, you trust!'

Beneath the palms, the laughter rolls,
Funny little critters with silly goals.
Swinging high, a monkey's flair,
Here's a riddle: Who's got the best hair?

Horizon's Echo in Serene Tides

Sunset splashes, colors collide,
As the outlooks dance on the tide.
Surfboards wobble as we all glide,
While fish cheer, but they can't ride.

A sunset sipper spills his drink,
Spaghetti on boats? Oh, what do you think?
Seagulls laugh at your tightrope walk,
While pelicans join to have a talk.

Time to shout, 'Catch me a wave!'
But oh dear, look at my brave.
Tripping on rocks, not feeling spry,
The surf's got jokes—oh me, oh my!

Shells echo tales from ageless shores,
While seaweed tickles, oh what a chore.
Each wave departs with a wink and wave,
As we chase the sound and misbehave!

The Call of the Coastal Symphony

Seagulls squawk in harmony,
Dodging crabby little crabs.
The clumsy dolphin takes a dip,
While the beach towel steals the tabs.

Palm trees dance with goofy grace,
As sandcastles totter and fall.
A crab in shades, what a sight,
Chasing shadows, having a ball.

The surfboards laugh on the shore,
Their wax is melted from the sun.
A surf instructor trips on a wave,
Claiming victory with a pun.

Chasing waves, life's a silly show,
As beach bums snooze without care.
A seahorse sips on coconut,
Who knew fish could party and share!

Cascades of Light on Azure Depths

The sunbeams play tag in the sea,
While fish chase bubbles that giggle.
A turtle reads a leadership book,
Clearly struggling with a wiggle.

Shimmering shells hold secrets tight,
Each one's a whacky surprise.
A clam wears a pearl as a hat,
Preparing for life's next disguise.

Octopus juggles seaweed snacks,
Making a show for the crowd.
Starfishes cheer with unglued limbs,
The antics are wild and loud.

At night, the moon's a disco ball,
Neon fish join in the fun.
They leap and twirl, it's total chaos,
Under the stars 'til the dawn.

Beyond the Oyster's Shell

In a reef of joyful chatter,
Oysters giggle in a line.
One shouts, 'Hey, who lost a pearl?'
'Not me!' they chorus, drunk on brine.

A starfish declares it's life's last dance,
While jellyfish float without a care.
A clownfish wears a polka-dot suit,
Reliving moments from the fair.

They play bridge over coral cracks,
Where fish tell tales of the stray.
'I saw a scuba diver,' one brags,
'But he looked lost and dismayed!'

With bubbles rising, laughter flows,
A sea cucumber triplets rhyme.
Underneath the briny blows,
They'll party like it's 1999!

Raindrops and Ripples at Sunset

Raindrops glisten like shiny discs,
Bouncing from the waves to shore.
Puddles form on sandy toes,
A race? Who could ask for more?

The sun dips low, a molten ball,
Surfboards foam with splashes bright.
Flip-flops slip in the muddy giggle,
While the tide waves goodnight.

Crab races forward, it's a sight,
Against a snail for a gold.
The crowd in shells just can't believe,
Wins are tales often retold.

The sea and sky unite in jest,
As the clouds wear silly hats.
A shrimp reveals he loves to dance,
The party must never fall flat!

Harmony of the Evening Tides

The seagulls squawk, making a fuss,
As crabs dance a jig, causing a rush.
The waves play tag, rolling on by,
While fish wear hats, oh my! Oh my!

A flip-flop flies, lost in the breeze,
With laughter erupting among the trees.
The sun wears shades, with a wink it beams,
While beach balls bounce on everyone's dreams.

The dolphins giggle, tossing a beach ball,
As surfers attempt to not take a fall.
A sandcastle towers, but wait one more,
A wave takes it down—oh, it's just a chore!

With each splash and cheer, the laughter grows,
In this whimsical world, anything goes.
So join in the fun, let your worries slide,
In this merry place, where joy won't hide!

Colors of the Reef in Elysian Light

A parrotfish flashes its rainbow attire,
While sea turtles spin as if on a wire.
The corals chuckle, painted in bloom,
Creating a palette that brightens the gloom.

The octopus juggles with cheerful delight,
Dodging the nets like it's taken flight.
While anemones wave in a swaying dance,
Even the clams get caught in a trance.

A crab with a monocle, oh what a sight,
Hosts a grand party beneath the moonlight.
The shrimp serve cocktails, oh what a fling,
As fish in tuxedos begin to sing.

So dive in the laughter, let colors adore,
In an underwater world that's never a bore.
With bubbles and giggles all swirling about,
Who knew the ocean could make us shout!

Breezes that Sing of Distant Shores

The palm trees sway, strumming their tunes,
While sandpipers dance under gleaming moons.
With a whispering giggle, the breeze sweeps near,
Tickling the toes of those sipping beer.

A crab plays the flute, quite the surprise,
While pelicans put on flashy disguise.
The coconuts roll, causing a fit,
As waves join the fun, they just won't quit!

A windsurfing squirrel in shades takes a glide,
While seaweed sways, a funky guide.
The umbrellas fumble and flip with delight,
As everyone bumbles into the night.

Each gust brings a chuckle, a laugh made of cheer,
Sailing through breezes that tickle the ear.
Join in the dance, let your spirit explore,
In this magical breeze where we all want more!

The Taste of Salt in the Sunset Air

The sun dips low, painted orange and pink,
As seagulls gather, giving a wink.
With salty snacks and giggles galore,
The beach BBQ is bound to floor.

A crab wearing shades nibbles on chips,
While sand castles tremble with all the flips.
The breeze blows in with fresh, salty cheer,
Mixing laughter with every "Ooh" and "Oh dear!"

A dolphin comes by, wearing a cape,
As folks stand around in a quirky shape.
The piña coladas take center stage,
While the sun sets down, flipping the page.

With snacks in hand, we toast to the night,
In this magical place, dolphins take flight.
So relish the flavor, both merry and bold,
As the sun's last giggle makes memories gold!

Indigos and Turquoises Unite

In a hammock that sways with glee,
A crab plays cards, sipping his tea.
Seagulls squawk tunes from the sky,
While dolphins dance, oh my, oh my!

Beach balls bounce on a sandcastle throne,
A crab conducts with a royal tone.
Mermaids giggle, their tails shimmer bright,
As they plan a ball under pale moonlight.

Flip-flops flying in a wacky race,
A parrot's prize: a feathered grace.
Shells stacked high, a tower of fun,
Who'll be crowned as the beach day's one?

So come and join this silly spree,
Where laughter echoes, wild and free.
In colors so bright, all chaos in sight,
Indigos and turquoises unite!

Vagabonds of the Sunlit Sea

With a hat so large, it could take flight,
A sailor shouts, 'This feels just right!'
Octopus juggling snacks on a raft,
While a shark cracks jokes with a hearty laugh.

Wind in our hair, we sail along,
A mermaid joins in with a lively song.
Sea turtles wearing shades so cool,
While crabs send maps to a hidden pool.

Seashells whisper silly tales,
Of pirate pranks and friendly gales.
Our ship's a taco, oh what a treat,
As we dance to the rhythm of fishy beats!

Waves may crash, but we'll just cheer,
Vagabonds of joy, never fear.
With laughter afloat, we'll sail the brine,
In a world where every glass is fine!

The Silken Touch of Salted Air

A walrus wears a dashing tie,
With flippers raised, he waves goodbye.
The sunflowers dance in a twist of breeze,
While crabs clink shells, saying, 'Oh, please!'

Lazy waves play tag with the shore,
A pelican's snore is hard to ignore.
Seashells gossip, sharing the news,
As starfish laugh in their sparkly shoes.

Swaying palms join a wild parade,
With beachcombers laughing, unafraid.
Flip-flop flings fill the salty air,
As the sun shimmies down, everywhere.

So breathe in deep, let your worries be,
In this whimsical land where we're all free.
With each silly wink, let mischief inspire,
The silken touch of that salted fire!

Spirits of the Misty Isles

Ghosts of coconuts float on by,
With giggles that tickle the sky.
Banana boats drift, oh what a sight,
While iguanas play twister till night.

Misty waves giggle, tickling toes,
With starry-eyed fish in flamboyant clothes.
A limbo line at the beach ball bash,
As a parrot yells, 'Hey, let's make a splash!'

The sunsets blush, wearing vivid hues,
A pirate sneezes into his shoes.
With so much fun under a tropical dome,
These spirits of laughter, forever our home.

So bring your joy and leave behind strife,
In a land where the seas dance with life.
With mirth all around, it's hard to disguise,
The giggles and grins, the spirits arise!

A Symphony of Shells and Skies

The conch blew loud, oh what a song,
The crabs all danced, they can't be wrong!
A starfish wore a jaunty hat,
While seagulls laughed at a sunken cat.

The waves did shimmy, what a sight,
They tickled toes, oh what delight!
A dolphin jogged, so spry and fleet,
Chasing his tail with joyful beat.

Sandcastles rose, each one a tower,
With lollipop flags that bloomed like flowers!
A clam held court, the king of bling,
Waving to pals in a pearl-studded ring.

So gather 'round, let laughter flow,
In our seaside choir, the merriment grows!
Together we'll sing, till the sun dips low,
And the tide takes with it all our woe.

Footprints in the Surf at Dusk

With wobbly legs, we hit the shore,
Each wave a giggle, begging for more!
Footprints scatter like a silly dance,
Where seaweed wraps around my pants!

The moon peeks out, a round and bright
As the sand crabs plot their midnight flight.
A pelican bobbed, looked full of cheer,
Till it mistook my snack for its spear.

Seashells sparkled, like a treasure quilt,
Collecting laughter that the ocean built.
We played hide and seek with crabs on the run,
And lost our worries to the setting sun.

Oh, beachy nights with a goofy flow,
Where tickled toes find the salty glow!
Each splashing wave, a burst of play,
Leaves whispers of fun in the close of day.

Harmonies Above the Blue Abyss

A fishy tune from a surfboard choir,
As jellyfish waltz, they never tire!
Octopuses jive, with eight limbs to sway,
While clowns of the sea throw a birthday parade!

Parrots squawk, with a laugh or two,
While crabs do the moonwalk, it's quite a view!
Blowfish puff with a squeaky sound,
As our sandy pals frolic all around.

The breeze hums softly, a tickling breeze,
As shells create rhythms, they dance with ease!
A dolphin who sings, lost in delight,
Makes even the gulls giggle into the night.

So let's raise our voices in a sandy spree,
In this whimsical place, you and me!
Laughing at clouds that drift in the sea,
In harmony swaying, wild and free.

Cascade of Memories in Breathless Seas

Through splashes of lime and waves of blue,
We chased silver fish, so bright and true!
Each bubble a giggle, how they rise,
As jellybeans swim through colorful skies!

The sun wore sunglasses, oh what a sight,
While sea stars spun in sheer delight!
With towels as capes, we leapt like a breeze,
Creating a ruckus, as wild as the seas!

A treasure chest, just a bucket of sand,
Harboring laughs from this magical land.
Seagulls performed a cheeky ballet,
As fish rolled their eyes at our silly play.

So let's bottle this joy, lest it fade,
In a wink and a splash, together we made!
From sun-soaked days with gleeful screams,
To the echoes of laughter in our sunbeam dreams.

Sunlit Currents and Celestial Tides

Sandy toes and goofy grins,
The sun's a highball drink that spins.
Fish in shades of neon bright,
Swapping tales till the fall of night.

Crabs strut by in fancy shoes,
With every stomp, they steal the blues.
Seagulls squawk their off-key song,
Claiming beach as their dance floor all along.

Flip-flops fly like boomerangs,
While jellyfish do salsa flings.
In this comedy of waves and fun,
Laughter rolls like tides that run.

So raise a cup of coconut cheer,
Toast to the frolics we hold dear.
As we splash and twirl around,
Joy's the treasure we have found.

Serene Horizons in Aquatic Hues

In skies of blue with whipped cream clouds,
Sailors laugh in their mismatched shrouds.
Sharks in shades of polka dots,
Wear smiles in ridiculous knots!

Turtles glide with such finesse,
While dolphins play the game of chess.
They leap and dive, a sight to see,
As if they're hosting a comedy spree.

The horizon wears a silly hat,
As octopuses breakdance - imagine that!
Each wave a joke that makes us giggle,
Swallowed by the joy and a little wiggle.

A sunbeam tickles each waving palm,
While paradise sings its warm, sweet psalm.
With each splash, our hearts in flight,
We chase the whimsies of delight.

Dance of the Seafoam and Sand

The sea foams up in a frothy clout,
While crabs hold a party with all their clout.
Seashells throw their glittery shindig,
As we dance like we're each a twig!

Fishy friends throw water balloons,
While the sun hums its mellow tunes.
Mermaids giggle in rainbow swirls,
As the breezy air twirls and twirls.

Waves crash down with a jubilant shout,
While surfers ride the giggle drought.
Even the sunsets join the spree,
Painting the sky in vibrant glee.

So come on down, let's wade and play,
Where joy is found in splashes all day.
With friends and laughter, nothing could be grand,
This is the dance of seafoam and sand.

Echoes of Paradise Unfurled

A parrot sings in a funny key,
While monkeys swing from the tallest tree.
Tickled by breezes, waves take turns,
As laughter ignites like bright lanterns burns.

Coconuts fall with a comedic plop,
And islanders laugh 'til they drop.
Fishes swim in a conga line,
Making every undersea moment shine.

The palm trees sway with witty charm,
While crabs parade in a conga swarm.
With sun-kissed skin and mischief in tow,
We wade through puddles where giggles flow.

As day slips into a starry veil,
We gather 'round, sharing our tale.
In the echoes of this laughter unfurled,
We find a slice of our whimsical world.

Whispers of Distant Shores

The seagulls squawk with silly glee,
Stealing fries from folks and drinks with tea.
Flip-flops fly, they land in the sand,
As laughter echoes across the land.

A crab in a hat, he struts with pride,
Trying to dance, with shells as his guide.
Fish in pajamas swim by the reef,
While we sunbathe, that's our belief!

Waves crash like jokes in a comedy set,
Splashing with giggles, no cause for regret.
Every splash tells tales of a pirate crew,
Who lost their treasure, but found a shoe!

As dusk paints the sea with a golden hue,
We'll toast to the stars with a drink or two.
The moonlight winks, with a mischievous smile,
Reminding us laughter is always in style.

Bliss Under the Coconut Canopy

Beneath palm trees, we dance and sway,
Swatting the bugs, while we groove and play.
Coconuts drop, it's a fruity cheer,
One hits the ground and we jump in fear!

A monkey steals chips, he's quite the thief,
While parrots squawk like they're giving grief.
We trade our sunscreen for beach ball fun,
Then trip on a towel, oh what a run!

Shells like treasures, we dig in the waves,
Finding new friends, like silly braves.
A fish with glasses makes quite a scene,
In ocean spectacles, he looks so keen!

As sunset glows in hues of delight,
We watch beach bums in a frisbee fight.
With laughs and cheers, we end our spree,
Under the canopy, wild and free.

Poetry of the Wind-Kissed Waters

A surfboard's wobble leads to great falls,
As dolphins giggle, breaking the walls.
With every splash, we can't help but grin,
The ocean's a stage where laughter begins.

A jellyfish floats by, wearing a crown,
While seaweed wiggles as we splash down.
Octopus juggling would steal the show,
In this underwater comedy, we all know!

The breeze whispers secrets to the tall trees,
As sand technicians sculpt with the ease.
Kids bury dad, he's a sandy delight,
Till he wakes and shouts, "I'm a beach fright!"

Night brings stars, a winking parade,
As we giggle over the memories made.
In waves of laughter, we find our tune,
Celebrating life like a wild cartoon.

Kaleidoscope of Colorful Shores

The vibrant hues of flip-flops collide,
As beachgoers dance in a wild slide.
Ice cream drips like colorful rain,
With sprinkles flying, it's an ice cream train!

Crabs in a race, who will take the prize?
With shells for shoes, they sprint with surprise.
A sandcastle stands, a king with a moat,
Until waves come crashing, oh what a note!

Children with buckets, they sing out loud,
Building their dreams, making us proud.
A seagull attempts a daring swoop,
Stealing snacks at the edge of the group!

As daylight fades with a colorful flare,
We gather together, it's time to share.
With stories of snorkels and flops on the floor,
We laugh till we cry on the sandy shore!

Elysian Echoes of Sea and Sky

Seagulls squawk and dive for fries,
While sunburned tourists lose their ties.
A crab in shades, with style so grand,
Struts like a model on the hot sand.

Breezes tickle laughter from a kite,
As jellyfish dance, oh what a sight!
Shells sing humor, each one a giggle,
Even the starfish do a little wiggle.

Waves bump the beach with a playful smack,
While a dog chases waves and splashes back.
Sandcastles tumble like jokes gone wrong,
Yet still we laugh, all summer long.

So let's embrace this cheerful spree,
With salty hair and a sunburned knee.
The ocean's rhythm, a comical tune,
Where every wave hums June to June.

Laughter in the Misty Night Air

Moonbeams gleam on a fishy fry,
Where mermaids laugh and dolphins sigh.
A crabby dancer moonwalks with glee,
Mistakes the sand for the dance floor's spree.

Lanterns dangle, swaying with grace,
While fireflies join in the silly chase.
The night fills up with chuckles and cheer,
As shadows prance, no hint of fear.

A sandman forms with a goofy grin,
Investing seashells for a win-win.
The tide rolls in with a mischievous plan,
To tickle toes of every fan.

So raise your drinks under starlit skies,
Where laughter flows and worries size.
The night is ours for a silly dance,
In the misty air, let's take a chance.

Cascade of Colors in Tide Pools

Purple urchins play peek-a-boo,
While sea anemones wave, 'Look at you!'
Starfish flip and change their hue,
Life's a party; join the crew!

Tiny crabs in their armored shells,
Tell knock-knock jokes, oh how it gels!
A sea snail slowly makes its case,
While an eel gives a cheeky face.

The tide draws back, revealing the bright,
A rainbow of creatures, pure delight.
The ocean's palette, a riotous glow,
With colorful antics that steal the show.

So dip your toes in this vivid spree,
Where every glance is a jubilee.
In every corner, wonders and hues,
In our delightful, watery views.

The Lure of Infinity in Rolling Waves

Waves crash down, a laugh in disguise,
Surfboards glide like birds through the skies.
A fishy joke in the foam does rest,
Tickling toes is the ocean's jest.

Gobbly gulls steal snacks with a grin,
While surfers chase their watery spin.
Bubbles explode like fireworks bright,
In the ebb and flow of sheer delight.

Children giggle as they build and splash,
Chasing their dreams in each salty crash.
A mermaid waves, with glittering scales,
Reeling in laughter, she never fails.

So embrace the chaos, let the waves play,
In this comedy show, come what may.
With every swell that rolls our way,
Life's a funny folly, come surf the sway.

Chasing Shadows on the Water's Edge

The sun's a big old spotlight,
We chase the shadows right and left.
A crab decides he's on the run,
But trips on seaweed, what a mess!

Seagulls squawk like they own the place,
Stealing fries from folks' plates.
With sandy shoes and laughter loud,
We dance around like silly mates.

The waves are playing hide and seek,
While we all giggle, splashing back.
Oh look, there's Dad – he's in too deep,
That wave just took his snack attack!

A sunset hues the sky like paint,
The day ends with a joyful shout.
Next time I'll bring my water wings,
So I won't tire out, no doubt!

Beneath the Banyan

Underneath the giant tree,
We play a game of peek-a-boo.
A squirrel joins us with a grin,
His acorn stash is quite askew.

We spy the fish, they wiggle fast,
While frogs croak songs of silly fate.
A ladybug on my toe,
I swear it thinks it's on a date!

A coconut drops, thunk on my head,
I swear it whispered, 'Take a nap!'
But then my friends, they start to laugh,
A perfect day, no time for crap!

The breeze brings tales of ocean trips,
And we all dream of pirate gold.
Underneath the banyan's arms,
Kid fantasies forever bold.

Dreams Set Sail

We built a boat from driftwood scraps,
With sails of t-shirts, bright and fun.
But soon we find our grand ol' ship,
Doesn't float well, oh what a run!

A dolphin laughs, swims by so free,
It jumps and splashes all around.
We wave goodbye, our captain dreams,
But instead, we're washed ashore, how round!

Now seashells scatter near our toes,
We make a crown, each piece a find.
The ocean giggles with our fate,
As we ponder what's on the wind behind.

With some brave hearts and flip-flop cheers,
We'll dream again of sailing wide.
Forget the storms, let's spin and shout,
Tomorrow's waves we'll ride with pride!

Whispers of the Coral Coast

Beneath the waves, the fish all chat,
While crabs and clams gossip side by side.
An octopus rolls his eyes in dread,
Saying, 'These sea shenanigans can't be denied!'

The surf sings tunes of salty cheer,
As shells exchange their secrets bold.
I swear I heard a dolphin joke,
About a seaweed that turned to gold!

The sandcastles wink with glee,
A palace fit for kings, they say.
But alas, a wave just came along,
And washed our dream estate away!

Still laughter reigns as we rebuild,
With sticky hands and salty lips.
The whispers dance like sunset rays,
As we toast our shaky, flipping ships.

Dance of the Emerald Waves

The waves do a jig, they twist and twirl,
While clumsy surfers attempt a stunt.
With splashes loud, they fall like logs,
Who knew the sea was quite this blunt?

A sea turtle performs a slide,
And steals the show from our group.
We cheer for her as she goes graceful,
While we flounder like an old soup droop.

In the shallows, we splash about,
Playing tag with fishes, quick and spry.
Bikini tops go flying wild,
As we chase seahorses, oh my, oh my!

At sunset's cue, we pack our gear,
With salty hair and cheeks aglow.
'Next time, we vow, let's dance some more,
Who knows what else the ocean's got in store?'

Enchantment of the Fragrant Breeze

A coconut fell, right on my head,
I thought it was a bird, instead it fled.
The palm trees whispered secrets, full of cheer,
I laughed so hard, I spilled my drink, oh dear.

The mangoes rolled like marbles on the sand,
I tried to catch them, but they weren't so grand.
A crab in a tuxedo danced in delight,
Claiming the beach as his own, what a sight!

Giggling pelicans are fishing for fun,
They dive like clowns, one by one.
My sunburnt nose may not be a trend,
But I'll wear it proud 'til the very end.

With ukulele strums under the sky,
We'll sing of the sun, let out a sigh.
For in this paradise, with smiles so wide,
Life's a carnival, come let's take a ride!

The Lilt of Waves Against Coral

The waves hum songs as they tickle the shore,
A parrot squawks back, forever wanting more.
The sea turtles dance in a slow saunter,
While fish in top hats join in for the banter.

A jellyfish entered the dance with a sway,
With tentacles swishing, it just could not play.
The starfish were cheering from their rocky throne,
While sea cucumbers just stared with a groan.

I took a dip, oh what a splash it was,
Came out beaming, but got stung, just because.
Found out the sea wasn't so friendly today,
But I laughed it off—such is the ocean's play!

With laughter echoing along the blue tide,
We danced with the waves, no reason to hide.
For every splasher and every wave crash,
Reminds us all—life's a beautiful bash!

Dappled Sunlight on the Ocean Floor

Sun rays dapple like a painter's brush,
As fish play hide and seek in a rush.
I tripped on a seashell, who knew it would squeak?
"Don't step on me!" said the shell with a peek.

Seaweed tickling my leg like a tease,
Mermaids giggling, setting my mind at ease.
Starfish rolling their eyes, thinking it's cute,
As crabs with their pinchers applaud the pursuit.

A dolphin jumped with a grin so wide,
Slipping and sliding, enjoying the ride.
I tried to join in, but only got wet,
The ocean laughed back, what a silly bet!

With treasures sparkling beneath the sun,
Each glance reveals a new kind of fun.
So here I frolic, without any care,
In this sparkling world, joy fills the air!

Journeys Through Clear Waters

I hopped in a boat with a squeaky oar,
It wobbled and danced, but I wanted more.
The horizon teased me with its bluest hue,
While a fish winked at me, as if it knew!

Our captain, a parrot, who squawked with flair,
Kept circling round, but I didn't dare.
The waves gave a giggle, oh what a jest,
As we sailed along, on a treasure quest.

A treasure map? Or just a saltine meal,
"X" marks the spot for a picnic, I feel.
But seagulls swooped down, trying to nab,
My sandwich escape, oh, such a drab!

In clear waters, my worries just slide,
With laughter and joy, they take me for a ride.
For every splash and every quip we make,
Life's an adventure—let's dive in and wake!

Celestial Currents and Island Dreams

On a beach where laughter flies,
Sandy toes and sunburned thighs,
Seagulls squawk with endless glee,
Chasing crabs beneath the spree.

Pineapples wear hula skirts,
As coconut drinks quench the thirst,
Dancing waves tickle my feet,
Underneath the sun's warm seat.

Kites soar high with silly flair,
While sunscreen's everywhere,
Flip-flops flapping with a song,
In this paradise, we all belong.

Belly laughs mix with salty air,
Life is grand without a care,
In this realm of fun and charms,
We'll sway along, linked arm in arms.

The Language of the Windswept Isle

Whispers dance upon the breeze,
Tales of fish who tease with ease,
Parrots squawk in tones absurd,
While island folks just laugh and herd.

Coconuts conspiring schemes,
Rubber chickens in our dreams,
Each wave a joke, each tide a pun,
The sun sets, but the fun's not done.

Palm trees sway, they know the score,
Making faces, oh what a chore,
Flip-flop races make us squeal,
As we tumble, we redefine 'real'.

Bikinis worn in neon shades,
Matching towels turned into parades,
We laugh at life along the way,
In our jesting, we'll always play.

Melodies of Surf and Shoreline

The surf sings songs both loud and clear,
Bubbles pop as we all cheer,
Sandcastles, moats, monsters too,
Where all our wildest dreams come true.

Starfish toss twinkling high fives,
In this realm, the silly thrives,
With jellyfish dancing afloat,
And dolphins planning their next joke.

Ocean tales told by the waves,
Of lost socks and silly knaves,
With tides that break into laughter,
Chasing giggles, happily after.

Crabs in bowties strut the line,
With little boots, oh how they shine,
Under this roof of azure skies,
Every moment's a sweet surprise.

Flickering Lanterns on a Calming Sea

Lanterns float like firefly dreams,
Guiding boats with laughter screams,
As the moon plays peek-a-boo,
Splashes giggles, a frothy brew.

Noodles fly on ocean winds,
While the starfish plot their grins,
Sharks with hats swim through the night,
Trying to scare the seagulls' flight.

Every wave a playful tease,
Perfecting our sense of ease,
As barnacles hold comedy shows,
Clam shells hiding punchlines' prose.

With lanterns tossing light and glee,
Our shenanigans flow like the sea,
On this stage of mirth and play,
We'll dance until the break of day.

Journey of the Wind and Wave

A gust that tickles, a playful flick,
Goes wrapping around like a fun little trick.
The sailboat wobbles with laughter anew,
As seagulls dive in for a splashy interview.

Waves slap the shore with a giggly cheer,
While fish swim away, calling, "Not over here!"
Crabs scuttle sideways, a comical sight,
While sandcastles tremble with laughter and fright.

The sun throws a hammock, all cozy and bright,
Where sun hats are flying, oh what a sight!
Belts made of seaweed, not quite a trend,
Yet here on the beach, we all just pretend.

And as twilight dances with shades of deep blue,
The beach party starts with a conch-shell review.
Coconuts clink in their cocktail attire,
While laughter erupts like a bubbly quagmire.

Moonlit Reflections on Still Waters

The moon hitched a ride on a quiet balloon,
Slicing the dark with a soft, silver tune.
Frogs croaked along like they knew all the songs,
While fish rolled their eyes, not bothered for long.

The water's a mirror, with stars setting games,
Where shadows can dance, and nobody's shamed.
A duck quacked ensemble, a comical show,
With ripples like laughter, to and fro they go.

Candles are flickering, the night takes a bow,
Pirates in pajamas, they're on the prowl.
Silly shadows flip, a grin on the lake,
While mermaids complain, "Oh for goodness' sake!"

With night's joyful tricks and the moon in delight,
The silliness sparkles, oh what a night!
Yet in all the fun, one truth still remains,
Even the laughers sometimes seek refrains.

Secrets Whispered by the Breeze

A whisper went dancing through palm fronds so high,
Dropping sweet secrets from up in the sky.
It tickled the sails of a boat far away,
Spreading the gossip of all who would play.

The breeze gave a nod, as the flowers replied,
With petals like giggles, nowhere to hide.
And bees buzzing loudly, they joined in the jest,
Choosing which nectar's the very best guest.

But wait! There's a crab who heard every rumor,
And he joined the feast, flaunting all in the humor.
With claws raised in triumph, he strutted around,
Declaring his kingdom of laughter unbound.

Then came a riptide with splashes of fun,
Carrying tales of everyone.
As laughter erupted and echoed with glee,
The breeze carried on, oh so blissfully.

Wanderlust in the Sea's Embrace

With maps in our pockets and dreams in the air,
We set for an island where no one's a square.
Palm trees sway gently, a rhythmic parade,
While we dance on the sand in our whimsical trade.

The waves play tag with our toes on the run,
"Catch me if you can!" they tease, full of fun.
We tumble and giggle, with sunscreen on noses,
Exchanging bright smiles like bright, blooming roses.

The sun's a warm friend who teases with light,
While piña colada stars would dance in the night.
The fireflies giggle as they wink and they tease,
Spreading enchantment with a sprinkle of breeze.

So let's toast to the folly of wandering far,
Where laughter's a compass and joy is the star.
The sea's warm embrace wraps 'round every glee,
As we twirl through our lives, oh so carefree!

Over the Coral Reefs, We Roam

Bubbles rise, the fish all laugh,
Dancing in the coral's bath.
Jellyfish float, a silly sight,
In this underwater flight.

Starfish wave with carefree glee,
While crabs join in a jig, you see.
A porcupine fish strikes a pose,
Winking at us, who knows?

Seashells gossip, secrets they keep,
As underwater buddies leap.
We snorkel by with grins so wide,
In this oceanic joyride!

Oh, what fun in this briny brew,
Laughing as we swim, it's true.
With every splash, our hearts take flight,
The seas are full of pure delight!

Tides that Sing of Home

The waves hum tunes of days gone by,
Seagulls choir in the cobalt sky.
A flip-flop lost, it floats away,
Searching for a sunlit bay.

The shoreline's dotted with treasures bright,
A crab in shades, oh, what a sight!
Sandcastles standing tall and proud,
Until a wave says, "Not allowed!"

A dolphin jumps with flair and grace,
Splashing my drink, oh what a face!
Laughter echoes through the salty air,
Joy's the gift that we all share.

So here we stand, barefoot and free,
Singing songs of memory.
The tides roll out, but we'll return,
With every wave, our spirits burn!

Serenity in the Breeze's Embrace

The palms sway gently, side to side,
As children chase waves, joy implied.
A floaty hat takes flight with cheer,
Mischief carried on the breeze near.

Shells and laughter scatter around,
Where ocean secrets pulse and sound.
A hammock swings, a sleepy sight,
Crabs stage a dance, what a delight!

Sunburnt noses, the sign of fun,
Ice cream melting under the sun.
Flip-flops squeak, a joyous score,
As we giggle, wanting more.

Amidst the surf, let's lose the clock,
With every wave, our hearts unlock.
The gentle breeze, our laughter's tune,
In harmony beneath the moon!

Canvas of Sunset Over the Waves

Brush strokes of pink light up the sea,
As crabs play tag, oh what a spree!
A sunset's palette, wild and bright,
With each new splash, we feel so light.

The gulls are actors in a play,
Performing tricks in a breezy sway.
A coconut falls, giving a thud,
While we giggle, covered in mud!

Beach towels flutter like flags of pride,
As faces light up, joy amplified.
The sky transforms, a canvas grand,
While seashells play in the golden sand.

We toast with drinks, umbrellas in place,
As laughter dances all over the space.
With every wave that kisses the shore,
This sunset's magic leaves us wanting more!

The Horizon's Infinite Promise

A parrot in shades, quite a sight,
Sips coconut juice, feeling just right.
The waves they giggle, as if in on jokes,
While crabs trot around in their tiny silk cloaks.

With sandals and piña coladas in hand,
We dance on the shore, like we're in a band.
The sun winks down; it's a holiday spree,
Even the palm trees sway, feeling quite free.

Seagulls are squawking, a stand-up parade,
They tell silly tales of the fish they once made.
With fins like our laughter, so spunky, so bright,
They dive for a splash, and we're left in delight.

And as twilight drapes in its shimmering gown,
The ocean whispers secrets to the clownfish around.
We're all just fish out of water, you see,
Laughing and loving our salty jubilee.

Secrets in the Starry Night

Under the moon, we concoct a plan,
To sprinkle some fun, like confetti from a can.
With crickets as DJs, they scratch and they mix,
We dance like sea turtles, pulling our tricks.

The stars wear their best, they twinkle so fine,
Like jewels from the sea, in a coconut shrine.
We point to the constellations, making up tales,
Of mermaids with ukuleles and octopuses in gales.

The ocean giggles, making waves with laughter,
As we brave the night sky, chasing after.
Let's catch falling stars, use them as bait,
Maybe to fish out our destiny's fate.

With the waves as our friends, and night as our glow,
We'll laugh till the dawn, let the good times flow.
Who knew the night hid secrets so bright?
Just a bunch of ocean-goers under starlight.

Embracing the Dance of the Seafoam

A frothy white bubble leaps from the crest,
Challenging dolphins to outdance its jest.
We follow along, like a conga line crew,
With pineapple hats and a lychee or two.

The beach is our stage, we strut, we sway,
As sand crabs join in, they're on holiday play.
"What's your best move?" one asks with a grin,
"I can moonwalk and backflip, let's win!"

The sea's laughter bubbles, it gives us a cheer,
While fish watch the show from their sparkly sphere.
We leap and we giggle, splash drops in the air,
Our toes all tickled, floating without a care.

As the sun turns to orange, we take center stage,
With a final grand flourish, we'll end this sweet page.
In the seafoam's embrace, we'll forever find light,
Just beach bums in bliss, dancing through the night.

Under the Shade of Warm Breezes

Beneath leafy canopies, laughter takes flight,
As we sip on our drinks, the world feels just right.
A parrot mocks us, it jokes away,
While toucans trade quips, brightening the day.

The hammock swings low, we sway and we pound,
Together we make our own silly sound.
With the sun on our cheeks and smiles on our face,
"Who squirted the lime?!" becomes a wild race.

The breeze tickles softly, as paws start to prance,
We join in the jig, it becomes a wild dance.
Whispers of coconuts rustle above,
While seagulls deliver the punchline with love.

Oh, how we frolic, our troubles a blur,
Dancing with ostriches, laughing like a slur.
Underneath the warm sun, our giggles take flight,
In shades of pure joy, everything feels right.

Embrace of the Ocean's Caress

The waves dance like a silly clown,
They tickle toes, then swoosh us down.
A crab walks sideways, unsure of its way,
While I chase my hat that's gone astray.

Flip-flops flying, a seagull's delight,
It steals my snack, oh what a sight!
I yell, 'Hey bird, you cheeky thief!'
It squawks in laughter, beyond belief.

Salt on my skin, sand in my hair,
Sunscreen's stuck, a sticky affair.
I juggle coconuts, oh what a show,
But they roll away—there they go!

The ocean giggles, a bubble-blown sound,
I trip as a wave flops back to the ground.
With a towel tugged tight, I take a bow,
I'm the dance champion—here and now!

Reflections on the Sapphire Surface

A mirror shines bright, but it's not my face,
It's a fish in a tux, in quite the fine place.
With a wink and a splish, it beckons me near,
I giggle, thinking, what's the catch here?

A round jellyfish floats by like a blob,
Waving hello while I'm stuck in a mob.
I tumble and giggle, what a clumsy race,
While my friends take selfies with foam on their face.

The sunset spills gold like it's made of syrup,
While I try to dance, but just end up in a hiccup.
A wave gives a push, I'm caught in a swirl,
I scream in delight as I twirl and twirl!

Now the stars peek out, the sky starts to sing,
Fish throw a party—what trouble they bring!
I cheer for the night with sand in my snacks,
Caught in the joy of ocean's hijinks!

Ebb and Flow of Paradise

The tide rolls in, steals my flip-flop,
I chase after it, but oh, what a flop!
Other beachgoers laugh, doing their best,
But I'm swept away, caught in the jest.

A pineapple drinks, with an umbrella hat,
I sit by its side, amidst this chat!
The breeze tickles me, like a playful bee,
While waves do the tango—just wait and see!

Bubbles arise, like troubles in dreams,
I chase them just like I'd chase ice cream.
They pop and they fizz, what fun we all have,
Oh, the stories we'll tell! I'll forever be brave.

A hermit crab in a home made of shell,
Waves a hello, it's killing me swell!
We dance on the shore; it's a wacky parade,
Embracing the chaos that sun and sea made!

Heartbeats of Seagrape Trees

Beneath the seagrapes, I find a sweet shade,
The squirrels are plotting, a game they have made.
I join their alliance, all hands on deck,
As we snack on the fruit—what a comical wreck!

The breeze whispers secrets, tickling my ear,
While waves give a shout, as if they can hear.
The trees sway in rhythm, it's party time here,
Until I trip over roots, oh dear, oh dear!

A gang of crabs joins in for the fun,
They dance in a circle, one and all spun.
Laughter erupts as they slip on a shell,
Caught in the groove, oh, what a swell!

At dusk, the fireflies begin their parade,
Bouncing on laughter, their nighttime escapade.
I sit back and grin, feeling quite free,
With heartbeats of seagrapes, just you wait and see!

Mirages of a Beachside Reverie

On sandy shores where seagulls squawk,
I lost my flip-flop in a clam shell shock.
The waves keep crashing, a rhythmic beat,
While crabs dance sideways, light on their feet.

A coconut rolling, oh what a sight,
It bounced like a ball in the warm sunlight.
I chased after it, my hat flew away,
Now I'm the joke of the tropical play.

With sunscreen slathered in a messy smear,
I resemble a ghost, that much is clear.
The sunburn's coming, oh how it bites,
But laughter erupts under starry nights.

As laughter rolls in like an ocean tide,
We clink our drinks, let the fun be our guide.
Life's a beach, and I fit right in,
With mirages and giggles, let the games begin!

Kaleidoscope of Fish Beneath the Surface

Diving down deep, I'm a sight to behold,
With fins flapping wildly, I'm feeling bold.
The fish are a frenzy, a colorful crew,
I waved at a grouper; he just swam through!

A marlin flips and a crab gives chase,
While I'm busy fumbling, losing my grace.
A seal popped by with a cheeky grin,
He tossed me a seaweed, "Put that on kin!"

Bubbles escaping, I laugh as I sink,
I'm part of the show; that's the way that I think.
Look at the jellyfish, floating like blobs,
I hope they don't think I'm a part of their mob!

In this underwater clownery parade,
I perfect my dance, though I often mislaid.
With fins and flippers, oh what a sight,
My fishy mischief makes for a night!

Barefoot Walks Along the Briny Edge

Barefoot I wander, it's quite a feat,
As waves steal my sandals, oh what a treat!
I'm dodging the crabs with a hop and a skip,
While seagulls dive-bomb in a tactical trip.

The ocean calls me with a friendly tease,
"Wet feet are mighty, pure breezy ease!"
But while I'm prancing in an ungraceful whirl,
A wave greets me sharply, it's all a twirl.

I trip on seaweed, a most slippery foe,
Yet laughter erupts, this is how it goes.
I gather my bearings, with salt in my hair,
Chasing waves like a child, without a care.

The sunset's a canvas, painted in jest,
As I laugh at the water that's put me to test.
Every footstep, a story anew,
Barefoot adventures in the ocean's blue!

Moonlit Secrets of the Caribbean Dream

The moon beams down with a sly little wink,
As I fumble my way to the edge of the brink.
A crab finds my shadow and scuttles away,
This beachside blunder is quite the display!

Stars twinkle overhead as I trip on the sand,
Who knew that starlight could reach out a hand?
With a dance in my step, I sway to the tune,
Of waves giving secrets under the moon.

A coconut drink spills, oh what a delight,
As I slip on my laughter, it's a slippery night.
My friends are all giggles; we're plotting our scheme,
To ride a wave home, in this surreal dream.

The night wears on with mischievous glee,
As jellyfish glow like a disco spree.
With moonlit secrets that beckon and gleam,
We dance on the shore, living out the dream!

Lullabies of the Lagoon

In a hammock that swings with glee,
A crab sings a tune to a fish in a tree.
The water's so clear, I see my own face,
"Why do I look like a walrus in lace?"

With coconut snacks delivered by breeze,
I dance like a dolphin, oh what a tease!
The ducks in tuxedos splash on the shore,
Laughing at me as I roll on the floor.

The parrot cracks jokes, he's quite the delight,
His feathers all plumed and his eye full of light.
While iguanas play poker behind the tall grass,
I wonder who's losing — it's quite the fine class!

As twilight draws near and stars start to peek,
I'm serenaded by frogs, oh what a freak!
With laughter and splashes, the night's just begun,
In this silly lagoon, there's always more fun!

The Horizon's Embrace at Dusk

The sun winks at clouds, a cheeky old chap,
As manta rays glide by in a fancy nap.
A seagull flips burgers, what a sight to behold,
While waves brag about stories they've never told.

In this playful expanse, even stars take a dive,
Splashing in colors that seem to come alive.
The sun makes a face, as it tumbles away,
"Don't let the jellyfish steal my last ray!"

A clam starts to boogie, it knows how to sway,
While shells join the chorus and join in the play.
The horizon's so bright, with giggles and cheers,
Sailing in silliness, we conquer our fears.

As night blankets softly, a shimmer of light,
We dance with the waves, oh what pure delight!
Each burst of the surf, a chuckle or grin,
In this world of whimsy, let the joys begin!

Secrets of the Deep Blue Realm

Under the waves, where the secrets unfold,
An octopus knits with threads of pure gold.
He whispers to clams, "Now listen real close,
I'm making a cape for a jellyfish ghost!"

The turtles do backflips, they're quite the cool crew,
While fishes line up for a style rendezvous.
A shrimp with a trumpet recites a tall tale,
Of mermaids who swim with their pet goldfish snail.

The seaweed throws parties, the crabs bring the snacks,
While lanternfish glow with their bright little backs.
"Let's dance till we're dizzy!" the squid starts to shout,
While the whole ocean giggles, no fear of a drought!

In the deep blue abode, where laughter runs free,
Every secret shared, just adds to the spree.
So, dive in with joy and let silliness swell,
In this world of wonders, we all know it well!

Gentle Embrace of Ocean's Caress

A wave tickles toes on the soft sandy shore,
Where flip-flops are tossed, and laughter can soar.
A starfish holds court, regaling its fans,
With tales about surfing and brave ocean plans.

The sandcastles giggle, adorned with sea flair,
As sea cucumbers dance without a care.
A shrimp in my pocket plays hide and seek,
Kicking up bubbles, oh what a cheek!

Sunsets ballad sung, colors all stirred,
While dolphins serenade, rhythm preferred.
"Just jump in the waves, let the fun never cease,
Embrace all the silliness, let life be a fleece!"

As night gently falls and the moon starts to rise,
The laughter still echoes like sweet lullabies.
In the ocean's warm hug, we giggle and sway,
For life's a grand party in every way!

www.ingramcontent.com/pod-product-compliance
Lightning Source LLC
Chambersburg PA
CBHW052221090526
44585CB00015BA/1436